Faceboo For Beginners:

Learn How to Advertise, Market Business, Brand, Products and Services Effectively Using Facebook Advertising

By

Dale Blake

Table of Contents

Facebook Ads For Beginners: Learn How to Advertise, Market Business, Brand, Products and Services Effectively Using Facebook Advertising

By Dale Blake

Introduction

Digital advertising has been there for a while. With social media now commanding a big portion of modern day traffic, the number of entrepreneurs venturing into social media marketing has been on the rise. Even though this might sound simple and fun, the fact that you have to plan and convince makes it as competitive and challenging as any other form of marketing. Understanding the basics and all the related tricks is key to ensuring that you get your Facebook adverts right from the word go.

Understanding what drives Facebook ads, how people use Facebook is key to charting out the right marketing strategy. Any advertisement should not only pass the message but also appeal to the reader's senses. This will not only let you in on why you should try Facebook adverts but also give the tricks you need to survive and make an impact.

Chapter 1. Why You Should Try Facebook Ads

With Facebook ads you can make accurate calculations on your ROI with ease. Numbers do not lie and that is what you bet your money on when you invest a convincing amount of capital on this approach.

Facebook ads offer better market reach than other forms of advertising. Well, TV as well attracts a significant number of consumers every day. However, with the advances made on the internet have caused a change of tide. Research has shown that most people are opting for the internet to satisfy their needs. With the immense amount of information available on the internet, there is no better place to look for insight. Furthermore, access of the internet has become cheaper and more readily available than it was I the past. This can be attributed to the increase in number of internet-enabled devices that are portable.

Most importantly, the internet is a global village and the best place to capitalize on is where most people are congregated. In that case, no one can refute the immense opportunities that exist on Facebook and what better way to utilize this opportunity than by advertising using ads. With the kind of effect they offer, Facebook ads are extremely easy to notice. As long as you have a catchy logo, there is no doubt that you will have more clicks on your link. The only other thing you can maximize on is including content that is insightful and useful to consumers to ensure that they always come back.

Another reason why it is necessary to invest in Facebook ads is they are extremely cost effective. When you compare them to traditional forms of advertising, the amount of capital invested is quite negligible. The minimum amount you can spend on these adverts is just $1 per day. In that case, you can set aside a budget for your advertising to ensure that consumers are always aware of the existence of your company and at the same time increase your market to consumers who are oblivious of your activities.

Furthermore, with Facebook ads you can be sure to save on your company's expenditure. These ads have the lowest cost per 1,000 impressions. Facebook ads cost an average of $0.25 per 1,000, which is just 1% of what you would have invested by advertising on TV.

This is a lifetime deal and as a marketer, you should know that there is no other place you will get a better deal aside from this.

All these benefits and you do not even have to spend a lot of time managing the ads. The fact that they are viewed the world over, you can be sure that you are not appealing to the local market but to a larger global market. The only thing you have to avoid doing with Facebook ads is coercing people who are not interested in your brand to like your page. This might seem promising at the beginning but it has adverse effects in the future.

Chapter 2. Creating Your First Facebook Ad

Facebook has two major types of adverts. The news feed adverts and the right column adverts. Due to their prominence, the in-newsfeed ads tend to convert more than the side bar ads. Even though Facebook is working on making sidebar ads more convincing, learning how to create your first ad by creating an in-feed ad will ensure that your first campaigns yield the most fruitful results.

To create this type ads:

1 Create a Business Facebook Page

By now, you business should own a sleek business page. If you do not have that, use your professional Facebook account to create the page. This should preferably be in the Facebook account you will fund to create and maintain an advertisement campaign. A page is mandatory since this type of ads suggest posts from a page. In this case, they will post suggestions from your page.

2 Prepare your content

Before spending money on your adverts, you first have to be sure that your ads will work. You have to learn the type of posts that engage your readers to the fullest. Are they pictures or short posts? Do they fancy long posts with frequent images instead? Even though this will be a test run of your adverts, you must still ensure that the advert takes on the right format.

The main Offer

Go straight to the point. Tell us what you are talking about and grab our attention, make us want to click. If possible present your topic as a problem.

The solution

In this section, we'd assume that your first section was good enough and has got the reader this far. It is time to win their confidence by providing elaborate solutions to the problems you presented

Contact method

This will help you convert the people who came by into visitors. Tell them to call you, email you or visit your website.

Additional information

If there is anything you would like to say, this is the time and place. Just make it short and as objective as possible.

Call to action

This last bit of the advert will encourage the reader to comment, share or like. You could also put the visit my site or enter a contest link here. The more interaction you create the higher the chances of being effective.

Following this simple format when advertising your goods or services will ensure you pass all the relevant information to the reader in the fastest way possible.

The value of an additional image

Some advertisers value the true power of an appropriate image in your posts. Using something captivating and clear shows that you are creative and serious. You do not have to cram text into your image to pass the message across. This would be the work of the text in the post. After all, Facebook does not encourage images full of text in their adverts

Investing in an intuitive image that will pique the readers' attention is the most perfect way to using images in your ads. An image could be worth a thousand words. It is up to you to decide whether these adverts will be chasing away your potential clients or drawing them closer to you.

Chapter 3. The Anatomy of a Successful Ad

Advertising on Facebook is a promising business-marketing plan that is bound to materialize into huge returns. With Facebook, the numbers are available. The only thing you need to grow your company is a must-have product and content to back up its sale. Other than that, you can only wait and be sure that your market share will grow. Here are some necessary hand me downs that will guarantee a successful Facebook ad.

Most importantly, your website should be mobile friendly. This factor cannot be taken lightly especially when you consider the fact most consumers use their phone to make searches on the internet. Portability is more enhanced with mobile phones than PC's and that is why most people prefer them. Actually, 70% of Facebook users around the world have been estimated to be mobile users. With this figure, you can be sure that most people will get to know more about your company and services through Facebook.

Another thing you need to capitalize on is an ad image with a considerable size. This is an important factor, whether you are posting an ad on Facebook or on the paper. Your ad should not be too big or too small but just the right size. If you are not quite sure what size is appropriate for your specific ad, it is best to seek the advice of a consultant before making any choice. However, the best image size to upload is preferably 1200 by 627 pixels. On the other hand, Facebook recommends Facebook image sizes to be at least 600 by 225 pixels.

Additional aspects such as design also come into play when it comes to attracting web users to your link. Since the image of your company is the main attraction, you have to make it as convincing as possible. In that case, it is necessary to upload a photo that matches what you are offering. Make sure you choose the best photo you can get. In simple terms, if you can get a high quality photo, it would be better for your advertising goals.

Do not forget to include an offer where possible. Consumers are highly attracted by bargains and incredible deals. Therefore, by throwing in a couple of discounted price offers for some of your products, you will be sure to attract them to other products you have on offer. If you cannot manage to include an offer, there are other options- by including key benefits of your product.

Furthermore, you have to include your company's name. This is crucial and must be thought of keenly. Do not just include your company's name anywhere, ensure that it is mentioned at an appropriate place. This is perhaps the only way you can ensure that web users who view the image will recall your brand.

Avoid making your image too sophisticated. The image should be clear and easy to interpret. Since you are targeting different kinds of consumers, you have to ensure that they will have an easy time knowing what your company is all about.

Chapter 4. Important Things to Consider

The secret to attracting web users to your link is by giving them what they want. Offers, a useful product and insightful advice delivered in a catchy way is therefore necessary. With Facebook ads, the same approach should be applied. With the increase in number of web users - and most of them having a Facebook account –, it is easy to make the most of this platform to expand your market share. Some of the considerations you have to make when choosing a Facebook should center on creating a lasting effect.

Most importantly, your Facebook ad should be the right size. Since your ad is the main attraction, it has to be visible. Facebook recommend companies to use images that are 1200x628 pixels. In that case, before you upload your company's logo, make sure it fits with what Facebook suggests. You can be creative enough to come up with an add that maximizes on results regardless of the space.

Do not forget to include important details about your company. Your company's name should definitely appear on the image and it should be more conspicuous than the other details. Thereafter, you have to include important details such as key benefits about the product. Consumers need to get a taste of what your company is offering in order to be enticed to know more. Your contact number is also necessary to include beside the image. Web users are some of the most impatient people especially when you consider factors that sometime hinder their access to links they want to follow- such as slow internet access. For that reason, it is not out of the question to include your company's hotline number.

To enhance readability, you have to play around with colors. Avoid dull colors by all cost since they will only shun consumers away from your ad. Again, do not use colors that match what Facebook uses as its theme colors. Since people spend most of their time scrolling up and down to see what is trending, they will easily forget about your ad worse of all, fail to see it. Use brighter colors like purple, green, dark blue and so forth to differentiate your ad from the Facebook theme.

Think outside the box. It is best to come up with your own logo instead of relying on images downloaded from the internet. Take your time; do not rush to create an image for your company. Furthermore, do not come up with a sophisticated image that will be hard for web users to interpret. Do not deviate from the purpose of uploading your ad on Facebook, by trying to do so much. The most important factor is to offer maximum information to clients using the minimal space offered.

Have a target audience in mind when deciding on the kind of photo to use. Do not just come up with an image, take into consideration the age bracket of your target market then come up with your design.

Chapter 5. Testing Your Ad's Relevance

It is not enough to set up your Facebook ad and leave it at that. You have to test it to find out whether it is up to the task or not. Actually, some Facebook ads fail to deliver the intended effect designed for them and that is where demographics come along. Perhaps the major disadvantage we get with Facebook ads is you cannot count how many times each ad appears. Therefore, cases where one ad may appear more times than others have been common. Coming up with different ad sets has become very necessary. For that reason, companies should collect enough data points to enable them carry out a split test for their ad. A couple of variables can be used to make sense of the matter.

On that note, the first data a company can do is make two versions of the same ad and compare the performance each has. Facebook allows you to make up to 6 images for every ad and you can use this opportunity to choose one that has the greatest impact. You can change one aspect of the image in one ad and find out the kind of effect that will offer. Thereafter, you can use Facebook ad manager to get the results for the changes done.

In addition, you must have a couple of factors that measure the kind of impact your ad has on Facebook. At this point, it is necessary to know how to create Facebook ads and use Facebook ad manager. The Facebook ad manager is what will determine whether your ad has achieved the intended target or not. Therefore, you have to select one ad objective you are intending to achieve. Take the advantage offered by Facebook to make a good bid for your ad. If it is your first ad on Facebook, it is best to try out both the CPC and CPM to before making a final choice.

Another great idea you can apply to test your ad is by using demographics. This way you can target the movement of Facebook users who are interested in your company. In that case, you can use any of the available options that can be used to mix and match audience presence and find out, which ad has leverage over the other. Some of the aspects that can be used to differentiate Facebook users include age, gender, location, relationship status, purchase level, interests as well as more precise means such as email, phone number and so forth.

Furthermore, you can make good use of track-able links to find out who is interested in your brand. UTM tracking parameters come in handy at this point and if you are aware of how to use them, that will be an advantage for you. You can have a custom Bit.ly URL for each post to allow you to come up with comparisons for the different links you have. This will be a big boost in tracking how your post is performing.

Chapter 6. Benefits of Testing Your Ad

Testing the performance of your ad is perhaps the only way to grow your business. Split testing also known as A/B testing is a well-known performance test. However, while most businesses know the kind of effect it has, a majority of them do not make good use of it. In that case, this can be the kind of leverage you need to outdo your competitors. Split testing measures the response consumers have on the kind of content they release. Depending on the number of clicks you get for your site, you can easily tell if the public is pleased.

Most importantly, split testing enables companies to offer consumers improved content. Since split testing offers a chance to discuss and share ideas, it becomes easy to settle for the best one. Again, this method allows you to measure different parameters that are associated with consumer behavior making it possible to know the kind of impact different changes will have on your company's performance.

A/B testing can also promote allocation of resources to areas that are bound to maximize on a company's profit. It is easy to allocate money towards activities that are not bound to have any impact on your company if little or no research is done prior to making the investment. However, if you do your homework before opting for anything, chances are you will get better returns.

Split testing is also a great way of mitigating the risks your company might experience. As your business grows, so does the risks you are bound to face. However, testing potential customers before making a final decision is a great way to reduce the amount of risk the company will experience.

It is also important to carry out split testing especially of you are planning to introduce a new product into the market. So many factors come into play when you want to introduce a new product. Since you do not want to launch something that will not be accepted by consumers, it is best to do a meticulous search on the internet using this tool to find out the kind of response it will get.

Furthermore, split testing is a cheaper way of reducing the amount of expenditure your company is planning to have. There are different ways a company can test its products and how they are performing in the market, but none of them is as affordable as A/B testing.

A/B testing is also a great way of highlighting the kind of progress made by your company in time. Checking out the trends can enable you to figure out what you need to do to improve on your failures and successes. The best thing about it is you do not have to employ a large workforce to do the research.

Research has clearly shown that there is a huge difference when a company carries out its marketing strategies using A/B testing results. The reason why A/B testing is bound to work for you is that it represents what consumers feel about the product.

Chapter 7. Expected Returns per Facebook Ad Campaign

Facebook ads have some of the most lucrative returns ever. However, you have to learn that adverts are never the same. Your demographics, page popularity and the natural appeal of the content you choose to market will determine the success of your adverts. This, therefore, means that there are many metrics of ad success. It could be on the investment-returns basis, on the number of likes and shares you get or the number of people who take action on your call to action.

To avoid any complications and frustrations, advert testing on a small budget will help you know the marsh and puddles to avoid when you go mainstream. Start with a small campaign on a specific type of ad and content without any expectations. Let it run for a day or so before doing your analysis. Do people do many views with less clicks? Do they click and ignore your call to action?

The answers to such will help you optimize your adverts and draw an expectation whenever you go live with a bulky advert campaign.

On average, Facebook adverts are very impressive provided you choose the right content and audience. A perfectly set up advert will elicit the shares, clicks and hype you need to make it in your niche. A poorly set up ad will be frowned upon. It will never make it beyond the cycle of people who is as a promoted link. Since Facebook will never teach you how to make these awesome ads, it is your sole responsibility to learn the tricks before you launch.

Remember the side bar and in timeline ad difference

This difference is universal. Sometimes, it does not matter how good your advert is. Its location will have an influence on your returns. Moreover, investing in a Facebook page will give more flesh to your campaigns hence increasing on your returns.

Chapter 8. Setting Up a Daily Budget

With the testing, tweaks and optimizations out of the way, you can go ahead and schedule a budget. Your daily budget, in most cases, depends on the competition at the market. This means that at times, a home improvement advert to an audience in New York could be more expensive than the same ad to people in Chicago simply because the demand for such space is lower over in Chicago.

Your target audience's demographics has a great impact on the cost of the advert. With the Facebook ad planning tool showing you the estimated reach (impressions) per day with each budget, you can always tweak the demographics of your audience to get the click possibilities out of the venture. If you are confident (from your tests) that your ad strategy will work, then you can always choose as hefty a budget as you can afford.

Change to maintain relevance

As always, any audience is dynamic and impossible. People's preferences will ever be changing. If you keep to a fixed strategy, you will end up losing relevance in the market or perhaps lose your position to a better competitor. To avoid this, it is advisable that you keep analyzing your advert trends and making simple changes and tweaks whenever need there be.

Using Facebook's ad management center would be a perfect way of keeping in touch with what is going on. At this dashboard, you can see all the interactions that are in form of clicks, comments or likes and views arising from your advert campaign.

The other relevant feature to be on the lookout for here would be the audience peak time. Look at the daily trends graph and identify the time when you get the most hits out of the advert. This would be the best time to run the ad. There also would be times when it is at its worst. Pausing the advert at this time will help you maximize on your advert's reach without investing in a bigger budget.

Conclusion

Sometimes, you might have hire a professional advert manager to get the job started. At other times, taking some time to learn the basics could be all you need to get things up and running. Keeping your cool and trying to learn the ropes will help you unearth a couple of advertising tricks you would have paid a fortune for. Remember that the more the following you gather the more effective your posts will be. This is so since as your following rises, so does the number of people who see your ads.

This does not however mean that you can jump into it without learning the basics. Taking a couple of quick lessons will teach you the things that you must do, what to avoid. You will have a better sense of direction since you will have the backing of professional experience to help you through.

I want to personally thank you for reading my book. I hope you found information in this book useful and I would be very grateful if you could leave your honest review about this book. I certainly want to thank you in advance for doing this.

If you have the time, you can check my other books too.